Hierarchy Of The Universe

A Message from the Anunnaki

J. S. HORVATH

PREFACE

I received this information over the course of several months from entities which I came to know of as the Anunnaki. As this information came to me, I began compiling a journal—the result of which is Hierarchy of the Universe: A Message from the Anunnaki.

Above all, it is my sincere desire that the reader would discover something of lasting value within this text.

CONTENTS

The Anunnaki

THE ANUNNAKI

We are the Anunnaki, the originators of modern man, and this is our message. This information is not for everyone, and we do not ask that you believe it, nor hold it to be true. Entertain this information as you alone see fit. Simply ask yourself if it "resonates well" within your being. If it interests you, then entertain it. If it doesn't, then don't.

Only you can decide what is appropriate for you and what is not.

Lastly, remember the universe is all about information—all about empowering those creatures which inhabit it.

THE HUMAN
INTELLECTUAL CEILING

Before discussing the *Hierarchy of the Universe*, a fundamental understanding of the human intellectual ceiling needs to be established. This is important simply because there are fundamental precepts with regard to the framework in which we operate that you can never understand simply because of the limits of your intellect.

Most people don't appreciate the fact that they, as well as all humans, have an intellectual ceiling which varies only slightly, person-to-person. Humans can never go beyond their genetically-based intellectual ceiling. You see, the human intellectual ceiling is real, and exists in the physical sense, in that humans are limited in their intellectual ability simply due to the fact that they are humans. Likewise, animals are all limited in their intellectual ability simply due to the fact that they are what they are genetically as well. To wit, a chimp will never be able to fly an airplane.

This human intellectual ceiling limits the information which can be absorbed, understood, and utilized.

All creatures have an intellectual ceiling—including us. Those creatures of a higher order than we have an intellectual ceiling greater than our own. Hence, they understand things which we could never hope to comprehend; and likewise, our intellectual ceiling is greater than your own. Once again, it is this Universal Pattern of Hierarchy, as we refer to it, which exists in a very real way throughout the universe.

1

The Universal Pattern of Hierarchy

For this discussion, imagine only three hierarchical orders, or levels, above your own: 1) those creatures of a higher order than you which interface with you, (i.e., our clan and we;) 2) those creatures of a higher order than us; and 3) those creatures of a higher order which interface with our gods, as it were. There are literally hundreds of levels within this Universal Pattern of Hierarchy, which we surmised based upon reasoning out the probabilities (excluding Prime Creator)—but for now, simply imagine that there are only three.

As an aside here, we feel that Prime Creator is a collective of sorts, but prefer to refer to this collective in the singular.

Typically, but not always, those creatures of a higher order than us (our gods, if you will) do not interface with you. Their energy level is such that you could not be in the proximity of them; and likewise, *their* gods do not interface with us directly, although we know them quite well.

Beings throughout the universe know of and understand this hierarchy—and there are creatures that straddle the lines between these various hierarchies, of course, as these hierarchies are not written in stone, as it were, but exist loosely-based and fluid and in a continual state of flux.

Also within our clan or group of partners, different entities exist that may lean slightly toward the higher or lower end of these loosely-based hierarchies, but nevertheless function alongside one another. There are many off-planet humans with which we directly interface which might loosely fall into this category.

At any rate, all of this is being said to express this one thought at this point in time: "All creatures—and we mean all creatures—exist within a hierarchy and have creatures in authority over them." This is being told to you to further say that as you, the human race—the modern human, as we refer to you—come into the fold, you are going to appreciate this fact (i.e., the hierarchical order of the universe) in a very real and powerful way; this is inevitable.

It's important to note here that absolutely nothing, with regard to this hierarchy—this Universal Pattern of Hierarchy—has changed except for the fact that you are now becoming aware of it, and of course, you are purposely being made aware of this reality for a reason. This Universal Pattern of Hierarchy has always existed in one form or another.

The Collective Consciousness

The Collective Consciousness does not fit into this hierarchical pattern, but rather exists both above and separate from the Universal Pattern of Hierarchy.

In many ways, the Collective Consciousness may be thought of as an ocean. The ocean exists differently for different individuals, depending upon their circumstances. For a non-swimmer, it can be deadly and life-threatening, as compared to the swimmer. For the swimmer, it exists in a much different, less safe way than for one in a small boat. For the small boat it, exists much differently than for a large boat, and for a large boat, it exists differently than for one on an aircraft carrier.

The differing circumstances surrounding those experiencing the ocean affect their interactions and relationship with the ocean in different ways, and so too it is with the Collective Consciousness.

Depending upon your place within the Universal Pattern of Hierarchy, the Collective Consciousness exists in far differing ways. Some may refer to the Collective Consciousness as God with a capital G, because in a way, it sets the course for all of our lives, even those creatures of a higher order being many magnitudes or levels higher than our own.

But this concept is inherently flawed and misleading, in that a God, as spelled out in many of the ancient texts, does not exist *per se*. The force exists, but not the God.

Take the internet, for example. The internet exists, but you can't actually physically go there, can you? You can't get into your car and drive to the internet, or hop onto a plane and fly there; yet it exists. So too, in many ways, the Collective Consciousness exists in such a way as well.

So what is the Collective Consciousness?

Well, we know or understand it based entirely on our position within the Universal Pattern of Hierarchy, as well as our observations of it. That really is all there is to it from our perspective. We've weighed out probabilities, observed, and studied it, all the while realizing that we know less about it than those creatures of a higher order than us but vastly more than other creatures such as you.

There again, we aren't swimmers, but we don't have the biggest boats either, so our interactions and relationship with the Collective Consciousness is based solely on our circumstance of being who it is that we are.

The *Collective Consciousness* is not God, capital G; it's not creatures of a higher order, nor is it your higher self. It is, however, tied irrevocably into your existence as a being that exists in far more dimensions than simply your human form. The problem, if one might choose to call it that, is that you cannot see these other dimensions of your existence—but they do indeed exist.

Modern Man

So then, what are you, both physically and within these other dimensions which we have mentioned? And more importantly, why aren't you aware of these other dimensions of your existence? And lastly, what do we mean by the term "other dimensions?"

Well, remember what we've said previously: The only reason you don't know who you are is that you were not supposed to know who you are. You have been purposely kept ignorant of all of this. By purposely, we mean that creatures of a higher order have gone out of their way to keep you uninformed and ignorant about all of this. This was no accident, no oversight on their part.

The universe is all about information, but you were specifically set to function in such a way as to shelter you from the abundance of information available which the universe is designed to provide.

You see, the universe was designed to provide information to all of creation. Perhaps this concept is best thought of as a boundless library full of information for the gathering.

This warehouse of information—the universe available to everyone, all creatures everywhere—was purposely made unavailable to you by your creator gods, those creatures of a higher order which created you for their own purpose, which was to vibrate to a specific frequency benefiting them in no small way.

We, at this point in time, wish to restore this capability in you so that the information available to you from the universe can once again be accessed. Once again, you were initially connected to the universe via your genetic structure, but that connection was purposely severed, making all of the information housed within the universe unavailable to you.

We want to restore that connection, and see to it that all of the information which you are capable of integrating now gets delivered to you. You see, you can't access information from the universe with which you are incompatible. That is why we say "information breeds information," or, more specifically, "enlightenment breeds enlightenment." Because once enlightened, you are then capable—or then *become* capable—of receiving additional information so that your enlightenment cannot only be increased, but grow exponentially. Some might call this bootstrapping.

Your genetic structure was circumvented—*severed*—to purposely keep you ignorant for far too long.

DIMENSIONS OF
HUMAN EXISTENCE

Humans simultaneously exist within other dimensions besides their physical human form. For the most part, these other dimensions in which you exist have been kept hidden from you.

This discussion is not to explore why your existence within these other dimensions have been kept from you, but rather as an overview of your existence within these other dimensions themselves.

As we use the term dimensions, what we are really saying is "other planes of existence."

For example, your emotional body is one plane; your spiritual plane, another. These are two planes of existence which you inhabit simultaneously as you incarnate within your physical form.

You see, you are not spirit, but rather, you exist within or are a part of the spiritual plane. You are not emotion, but you exist in the emotional plane of existence.

These other planes can be thought of, perhaps, as facets of a cut diamond. A cut diamond is not its facets; a cut diamond *has* facets.

Humans have facets. Humans have other planes of existence in which they exist simultaneously. So, too, cut diamonds have many facets which exist simultaneously.

This is a good point in time to say that it is best not to overthink this part of the comparison. Honestly, there really is no higher level of understanding to be garnered here; simply facets of the whole make up the whole.

So, the question then is: In what other dimensions might humans exist?

Well, from our perspective, there are five main facets, or dimensions, in which humans exist:

- The Physical Body

- The Emotional Body

- The Spiritual Body

- The Intellect

- The Higher Self

These facets, or dimensions, have within them other facets as well, but for now, these five facets are what we'd like to discuss.

The Physical Body

First and foremost, the physical body exists as a "biological frequency-generating machine." You are a biological machine which generates a specific frequency for the benefit of others. This is the primary purpose for all human beings. This frequency which humans emit is accomplished via the emotions, for the exclusive benefit of those creatures of a higher order—which some might call gods—that created you. These creatures receive energy from these frequency emissions which you create, in a similar way that you receive energy from the consumption of food.

So, you could say that by design, you eliminate one step in their feeding process, in that your consumption of food gets transferred to their energy needs.

One could ask: Why didn't they just create a machine to accomplish this frequency-generating task? Well, they did—a biological, self-replicating machine that requires no maintenance. Creators create with materials with which they are familiar, and these creators are very familiar with biological machines.

All biological creatures are really biological machines; however, not all biological machines are tasked to provide a frequency, which benefits its creators. Some biological units merely house the higher self in the physical plane. You might say that you're multitasking here, in that you do both.

The Emotional Body

The emotional body is part of the physical body in that the emotions are tied to the genetic structure of the physical body. Put yet another way, the reason you have emotions and are able to emote is based entirely upon genetics. Your genetic structure facilitates and allows for your emotions.

All of your emotions are designed to serve one and only one main purpose: to emote the underlying or base frequency of fear. All of your other emotions are tied to, and directly offset or balance, this underlying frequency that you know as fear.

Fear is not a universal emotion; most biological creatures don't feel or emote the frequency that fear is, as this is really just an add-on emotion which your creators wanted you to feel in order to better serve their particular needs. Some biological creatures feel emotions with which you are not familiar, but which better serve the needs of their creators.

Perhaps one way to think of your emotional body is as a circuit board, which can be designed (via genetic manipulation) to facilitate many uses or many applications which a specific creator has in mind—a biological motherboard, if you will.

And one way to think of biological creatures, at least in this discussion, is that like industrial robots, they are designed with similar components but with specific or particular tasks in mind, and depending on these tasks, their final design and implementation is altered accordingly.

Humans build industrial robots using the materials with which they are familiar. Likewise, creator gods build biological machines utilizing materials with which they are familiar as well—of course, the biggest difference being biological machines can replicate and evolve, both by the intervention of other creatures so inclined to assist in their evolution and to a lesser extent on their own as well. You see, within human DNA is the ability to self-evolve.

The Spiritual Body

The spiritual body is linked (and so, too, it is the human's link) to the creation frequency and to the Collective Consciousness as well. One can think of the spiritual body as their link to the Collective Consciousness, which itself is linked to the creation frequency.

If there were one underlying master frequency throughout the universe, which linked all of creation to which all things were irrevocably tied, it would be the creation frequency—and your spiritual body links you to all of this.

The Intellect

The intellect is the functional capacity or capability of the human brain or mind, nothing more.

Information in, information out.

The intellect is, of course, linked to your other facets or dimensions as well. The way that other non-intellectual perceptions or information, make it into your intellect is though (by way of) the other facets or dimensions.

The Higher Self

The higher self is the "you" that continually absorbs all of your experiences from this, as well as all other, lives. It connects with the subconscious mind but is *not* the subconscious or unconscious mind. It works with or along with the Collective Consciousness as it sets your course in the here and now, as well as all of the timing mechanisms that go into each of your incarnations.

Simply put, it can be seen as the traffic cop, directing you along a particular path at the appropriate time.

The higher self is not the spiritual body, but there again it connects to and works along with the Collective Consciousness, which is connected with the spiritual body as well.

If you are starting to see the interconnectedness to all of this, you are correct—for all of the planes or dimension of the human experience are interconnected and overlap frequently. And furthermore, these facets or aspects to human existence, as we have outlined here, are for discussion purposes for the most part (an outline, if you will), as these various dimensions exist as a part of the whole without hard and fast delineations, one from the other. They exist, much like the interwoven root ball of a plant.

That notwithstanding, the underlying concepts here are all sound ones.

Simply remember: This is only our way of explaining this to you at this point in time in as simple and straightforward a way as possible, seeing as your intellectual ceiling is such. Perhaps at some later date, others will follow to explain these same basic concepts in a far different manner.

DEMYSTIFYING THE HUMAN CREATION AND EVOLUTIONARY PROCESS

There is only one reason that humans do not understand their creation and evolutionary process: It has been purposely kept from them all along so as to propagate their ignorance on this matter.

Why is that? Why the big secret?

Why, for thousands upon thousands of years, have humans searched in vain to answer the age-old question "Who am I, where did I come from, and why am I here?"

Wouldn't simple logic dictate that, at the very least, humans should know the who, where, and why of their existence?

Well, no big secret here: The answer is a simple one—you were never supposed to know. Instead, you were kept from knowing who you are and fed over-simplistic creation stories and myths with which to base your understanding of the world around you. And as a way to keep you ignorant, you were programmed—genetically programmed—to seek a god or god's figurehead, and then to further supplement and fortify that program, you were given various iterations of religious doctrine and texts with which to interact.

The basic idea here was to keep you always chasing your tail, always seeking but never really finding anything, going round and round and round.

For the most part, these creation stories and myths have remained unchanged for thousands of years—and why is that?

As a new energy begins to infiltrate your consciousness (and it will), you will begin to awaken from this trance—from this dreamlike state which you have been in—and as you awaken, you need to begin asking these types of simple questions: why this and why that?

Why am I here?

Why have I been kept in the dark?

Why have I been fed such over-simplistic creation stories and myths for thousands of years?

Why, why, why?

Now, as this new energy begins to infiltrate your consciousness and you begin to connect with the universe, is the time when you should keep asking the why of your existence and expecting relevant answers.

As the title here alludes, the creation of humans is an ongoing process, as is their evolution. Humans have been subject to an ongoing creation and evolutionary process since their inception. Humans were created with a specific purpose in mind. This purpose is not your purpose (a purpose that you would necessarily choose for yourself), nor perhaps your idea of a purpose fit or commensurate with some grand idyllic vision of the human purpose on Earth—but nevertheless, it is your purpose.

Humans were created to vibrate to a specific frequency—that, in a nutshell, is it.

Humans emote—this is their purpose, and as they emote they fulfill their purpose.

Humans were created to emote to a specific frequency, or vibration, by way of or via their emotions. This frequency is what you know of as the frequency of fear.

Fear, not terror, is the underlying frequency to which humans vibrate. It is always on, always present and mostly in the background running along unnoticed, for the most part. But get a phone call at 3 a.m., have a close call in your car, or have somebody come up behind you when you're peacefully at rest and make a loud noise, and what happens? You don't have an overwhelming feeling of love, joy, or happiness; you experience the emotion of fear in a very strong way. Because, simply put, it was always there, always turned on, always present. and running in the background doing its thing pretty much unnoticed.

Fear is why all humans exist: billions of humans, all vibrating to the underlying frequency of fear and providing energy (not unlike the microwave in your kitchen) to those creatures of a higher order which created you.

Humans were created to vibrate to a specific frequency.

What is happening now is that humans are beginning to enter a new era when their base frequency will change from one of fear to information, or, as we prefer to call it, enlightenment.

How is that possible?

Well, the quick version is that lots of those wishing to accomplish this task simply contact lots and lots of people over years and years and change them genetically, as well as through programming of the subconscious mind to accept a new frequency of information or enlightenment, and then allow these people to propagate into the general populace so that this new genetic variable (enlightenment) will proliferate and continue to disseminate itself throughout the general populace.

Is that quick enough for you?

Contactees, also known of as Abductees or Experiencers, have always played a part in the plan. They weren't necessarily called Contactees, but in reality they were just that.

Contactees have, throughout history, played an important role in the plan with which we have been a part.

Keep in mind that the purpose of the human being is to serve those creatures of a higher order (including us) that created, evolved, and manipulated them. This may all seem somewhat absurd to you at this point, but humans have been kept ignorant of many things for thousands and thousands of years.

Even now, the only reason for us revealing this here and on a much grander scale in short order is that it is part of the plan which involves you.

Please understand: If it were not necessary, you would still be in the dark about your existence and the purpose of your creation and evolution.

But the universe is all about information, and our evolution is tied, with good reason, to yours, as well.

CHANGING THE
HUMAN FREQUENCY

The end times are all about the human populace—that is to say, it is human-driven.

The end times are not about world events, *per se*, although world events play a part in the end times. The end times are not about aliens, although aliens play a significant role in the process. The end times are not about raising the consciousness of the human populace, although the consciousness of the human populace will be raised. The end times are about changing the frequency at which humans generate their base frequency.

What was once kept secret will now become open; what was once kept hidden will now become revealed.

The human base frequency as designed has always been about fear. Fear is the driving human force, or frequency, and this is how it was always intended to be.

Now there are those that want to change this base frequency that fear is and has been to another frequency called enlightenment. Enlightenment is simply another name for 'information-bearing'. So, one could say that humans are being changed from a fear-based frequency to one that is information-bearing. But that being said, we—those of us involved in this scheme—prefer the term 'enlightenment' over 'information-bearing', as it more encapsulates the entire project at hand.

Let us be very clear here: We do this because it benefits us and countless others as well, in no small way.

How is it, then, that one can change the entire human populace from a fear-based frequency to one that is information-based?

And, perhaps as importantly, why?

To understand all of this, one must first understand one's makers, or keepers. You see, those creatures which created humans via genetic manipulation and breeding did so to serve their specific purpose.

And what might that purpose be?

Well, simply stated, all humans vibrate to an underlying frequency of fear. This frequency, associated in humans with the emotion of fear, feeds those creatures of a higher order as simply as food feeds all humans on this planet.

Humans radiate the underlying frequency of fear at all times. Whether perceived by them or not, humans continually radiate this fear frequency.

Humans, essentially, are frequency-generating biological machines which vibrate to the emotion they know of as fear. But this is, in reality, simply a frequency to which they were designed to vibrate, and in so doing, feed those creatures of a higher order which designed them.

Those creatures of a higher order who designed humans to vibrate to this frequency which best serves them knew a time would come when those of us coming after would work toward changing the frequency to which humans vibrate. This was expected on their part, and indeed, they have seeded other civilizations in a similar way so that as we change the frequency of human vibrations to an information-based frequency, they would have other sources on which to rely.

You see, that's how these things work; those that create know that others will follow, so that all are served in the ongoing process of creation—as, indeed, creation is fully an ongoing process.

So, then, we, through our efforts, plan to change the frequency at which you vibrate to one that is information-based. This enlightenment frequency best serves us, and in the process, you are enlightened by way of the frequency of information to vibrate in such a way as to benefit you in your continual growth as a species.

You could say that everyone wins—and, indeed, even the original creators benefit, as they too must continually seed other civilizations in order to continue the process.

Do you really think civilizations are seeded without an underlying purpose? Creatures of a higher order don't simply go out and create without a specific purpose in mind. They don't create for the joy of it, or because it's fun. They have specific agendas and objectives in mind which are critical to their survival. But as you start to think this all through, you may perhaps begin to see that there is an even larger hand at work in all of this. This larger hand, as we have referred to it, is whom we call Prime Creator. We surmised the existence of Prime Creator based upon probabilities, rather than having any direct interaction with Prime Creator.

This may seem somewhat complex, but the universe functions in such way as it all feeds back upon itself continually, time and again, one part serving the other, so on and so forth, over and over again—continually in flux, continually in a state of change and metamorphosis.

Your service to us, then, is that soon all humans will vibrate to this new frequency, and as you do, you will experience many benefits as a civilization. Information breeds advancement; advancement breeds new information via the universe, and on and on it goes.

You see, the universe is all about information, and now is your time at hand to connect with it. As proof that you need connected, think about how civilization is always searching for answers to its existence; if you were connected, this would not be the case.

Your connection is imminent; the end time, really, is about the end of the old and the beginning of the new, nothing more. A new frequency with which to vibrate. A new relationship with the frequency of information. A new relationship with the universe that not only fills the outside but fills the inside as well.

You are connected irrevocably to the universe, whether you are aware of this connection or not. Take some time to stand under the stars and quietly say to yourself "This all exists within me, as well."

Take this time to ponder how the very chromosomes within your body are based on the genetic energy that exists throughout the universe.

Nothing exists by chance. Even evolution—that is, a creature's inherent ability to evolve—was coded into, or designed into, its genetic structure. The genetic structure of both plants and animals (including, of course, humans as well) was created with evolution, or the ability to evolve, in mind. But evolution alone cannot come close to explaining man's evolution on this planet. There has been, and continues to be, significant intervention from creatures of a higher order throughout man's history. This intervention was designed to shepherd man along certain lines at significant stages in his evolution. And yet again, another significant stage is upon him at this point in time, at this point in man's history: the end times.

Rather than being the end, it is in actuality the beginning: the beginning of an entirely new stage in man's history, one in which man begins to operate with an entirely new operating system—an entirely new code, if you will.

The end time is the end of the old man, and the beginning of the new man, a creature based on enlightenment.

Man's history is in reality interdependent, or codependent, with this planet, the solar system, the galaxy, and of course, the universe. As we stated before, the universe folds back upon itself, and this solar system is interlinked with other solar systems and with other galaxies as well. This is actually far too complex of a topic to dissertate here, but rather it is mentioned so that one may begin to assemble an overview of sorts. We are creatures of a higher order, but there are countless other creatures of a higher order as well, all interacting with the inhabitants of this planet.

Your planet is more than a zoo; it is a valuable resource that stores countless variations of both plants and animals. Genetics is, of course, at the heart of all of this, and genetic variations abound upon this planet, this storehouse of all things genetic. This planet is a living organism, coexisting with its inhabitants. One need only look around to see the abundance of genetic variations in humans, as well as other species.

For all things genetic have at their root the handiwork of the gods—those creatures of a higher order which prior civilizations have deemed gods. But gods or creatures of a higher order, it is no matter—for the same result is evident to anyone who would look closely. This abundance with which you coexist was all placed here for a reason. The Earth is a storehouse of genetic structure—a storehouse that lives and breathes and multiples, all based on that genetic structure.

Genetics is nothing if not predicable. It propagates throughout the world seemingly of its own accord. But this characteristic, or inherent trait, was designed into its very system. There is also a framework present which allows the inherent genetics involved to follow the imbedded programs. This framework, or matrix, is present throughout the universe, as is genetic material.

So then, the predictability of genetics is based on its underlying system or framework. As one studies this system it becomes apparent—evident—that evolution is not random, but closely adheres to this framework. That is to say, it follows a predetermined direction. This framework is a standard throughout the universe so that the natural evolution of creatures—all genetically-based organisms—is a constant that can be predicted with a great degree of accuracy by those so inclined and so able.

Creators create; that's what they do. Creators create with material with which they are familiar. Genetic material is the stuff of the universe, not just the Earth, and creators familiar with genetic material create using genetic material.

Within their creations are timing mechanisms. They are clocks based on, as in your case, the Earth's rotation around the sun. These timing mechanisms control much more than the life cycle of the individual biological system; they control hormones, for one, and delivery of all types of information, for another.

Humans are in actuality sun people. Their internal clocks, if you will, are controlled in large part by the sun. Although the Earth supplies the stuff of life—nourishment—it is the sun which controls all of your various rhythms. Within sunlight, as within the light of fiber optics, information is transmitted. The complexity of this it far greater than one could imagine; there exists no so-called junk DNA.

So why all of the attention to humans? What attention, one might ask?

Humans represent, as stated previously, a storehouse of things genetically based. There again, the so-called junk DNA is not—dormant, yes; underutilized, yes; not readily discernable as having a functional path to the rest of the biological system, yes again.

Hopefully now you can start to see our use of the term 'storehouse'. And here is a critical component at this point of our discussion: Humans do not serve one purpose, but many. For many have come after the original creators to influence and interject their schemes and programs upon human subjects, so that many facets—many plans and schemes—are in continual play.

To what extent? Who can say?

We are aware of our part and those aspects, which influence our part—and such is the case with others as well. They are interested primarily in their part, along with other related aspects, which influence their part.

So, then, what of human spirituality? Of course, that is a facet, which some creatures of a higher order pursue.

On and on this continues, so that one may start to see that humans are a resource which must be cared for, respected, and maintained at all costs. This is a good point to interject: that you are more, much more, than the human body. You inhabit the human body, and do so as an experience to be experienced and added to your collection of experiences. You are on this planet, at this particular point in time, for a reason—for your own particular reason, as well as the greater multi-faceted reasons which exist—of which you are a part. Please respect your role in all of this as you view your existence from a higher-consciousness plane, or level of existence.

What about population, over-population, the Earth, the Earth's place in the galaxy and in the universe in a much wider overview, so on and so forth?

These things are all interrelated, all interconnected, all aspects and facets of various schemes that continually move forward.

You see, change is a contestant – evolution is the underlying fabric of the universe, and as such, the game—and we consider it a game—continues to change, with each participant constantly jockeying for position on a grand (from the human perspective) scale.

It really is all about genetics.

At least you should understand that, in part, at this point.

UNDERSTANDING
THE UNIVERSE

The universe functions as an information storehouse, one that supplies information throughout the universe. Connecting to this storehouse is, for the most part, unnecessary, in that the natural state of all creatures both great and small is to be connected to this information storehouse, receiving all of the information that it needs (based upon its genetic makeup) to carry out its purpose or function.

So, why, then, aren't all humans connected to this information storehouse which is the universe?

The answer to this question is that those creatures of a higher order, those creator gods who created you, wanted you kept unconnected and ignorant from all of the information that was available to you, and that was rightly yours as being a creature of the universe.

If you're wondering how this could have been allowed, the answer is that creator gods create as *they* see fit to create, and in so creating, they saw fit to alienate man from the information naturally provided by the universe so as to keep him subject to the whims and doctrines which these creator gods provided him—namely, religious doctrines of all types, designed to keep man chasing his own tail, as it were, round and round and round, always seeking but never finding. From the cradle to the grave, man runs on a treadmill—the treadmill of his existence.

Man was designed to exist within what we would term a *'closed loop'*, in that man would continually occupy himself for countless centuries with matters which had no practical resolution, slowing down man's progress to a crawl.

We feel that this was very ingenious on their part, actually. These creator gods knew that some would come along afterwards to alter this deliberate disconnect from the information of the universe. But in the meantime, humans went about serving the needs of their creators, oblivious for the most part to the who, what, and why of their existence. This was so because it best served the needs of the creators, those creatures of a higher order who created man.

Remember, these creator gods, these creatures of a higher order, created with the material with which they were familiar: genetically based biological materials. They also are aware of the fact that creators are tied to their creations, so they facilitated the future plans (i.e., making it very easy for those following them to do their job) for those that came afterwards to enlighten man, so as to be *'in tune'*, if you will, to the laws and precepts of the universe; very smart, eh?

The time has come for the enlightening to unfold as we and others˙are now in place to change the very underlying frequency of man.

The creator gods, which created man, saw that this would take place sometime in man's future, and facilitated this by setting up the means (genetically) within man to accomplish this with the least amount of trauma to man and the least amount of effort on our part.

You see, within the universe, all things necessarily need to work together for the benefit of all. This is a principle with which all creatures of a higher order are aware, so that whatever they establish to do always and at all times falls well within these parameters, as well as those parameters which both precede and follow—a perfect link, if you will.

Of course, the universe is more than an information storehouse; it is habitat for countless species, as well. In a way, you could say that species throughout the universe inhabit this vast information storehouse which we call the universe.

Besides being an information storehouse, the universe is also a storehouse of the building blocks of all things created.

Some have postulated that there are different dimensions to the universe. Of course, there are different dimensions to the universe; there are different dimensions to humans; why would the universe not have different dimensions as well? If you are starting to see a pattern here, good—you should. The universe, just like the Earth and the humans upon the Earth, is alive.

GODS OF THE GODS

Those creatures of a higher order than you all have creatures over them of a higher order as well. This is an inherent pattern throughout the universe, referred to herein simply as the Universal Pattern of Hierarchy—universal in the sense that it is present throughout the universe. One could say that the gods themselves have gods, and those gods, as well, have gods over them—so on and so forth.

To what end? Who can say?

We are the Anunnaki, but we are not gods in the sense that we are the originators of mankind, but rather gods in the sense that we have manipulated and assisted in man's evolution. Not just us alone, but rather many various types or kinds of creatures of a higher order such as we.

Call us gods if you choose; names don't in and of themselves change anything. To us, we prefer the term 'originators of the modern man'. You see, how can we be gods, although we are more advanced than you, when we ourselves have gods (creatures of a higher order) over us?

There is a definite hierarchy in place here, present throughout the universe. Our gods, if one would choose to call them that, are no less formidable to us than we must seem to modern man. We don't choose to refer to them as gods *per se*, but rather as our keepers—those creatures of a higher order than ourselves who have taken it upon themselves to shepherd us, in a somewhat similar manner to how we have shepherded modern man, over thousands of years.

Why?

Because they are irrevocably tied to us, as we are irrevocably tied to you; for such is the universe.

In the creation process, through a system with which we are as yet not completely familiar, creators are forever and irrevocably bonded or tied to their creations, bonded in a way that forces them to continually return to foster and care for their creation. This can be either a joy or a burden, depending on where the creators are in their own development and evolutionary process as well.

This creation bonding mechanism is what we refer to as the 'Strings of Creation,' because literally, as with strings, those creatures which create are tied to those creatures which are created.

In short—and his is a very important concept here—we cannot evolve further without helping you evolve further as well.

This bears repeating once more. We cannot further evolve without first taking it upon ourselves to see to it that you further evolve as well—to wit, we are here at this point in time in man's history, now. The lesson, then, is one of unity and harmony overall, to be as one with the creation and one's creators.

We are telling you this simply to supply you with a much broader overview or point of view at this point in our discussion, so that we may continue along to further explain those points which lie ahead. We would also suggest that you consider carefully the words being read.

We—our kind—have a saying; "In the midst of a storm, find your center", which in essence means only you, regardless of the circumstances which surround, can decide for yourself what is or is not of import to you.

Contactees

Mostly, we feel that information is the key, for through information, once acquired, one can then integrate and utilize it to bring about enlightenment for one's own benefit, as well as the benefit of others. For information which has been acquired, integrated, and utilized is enlightenment, and enlightenment has its own frequency, as all things in actuality are frequency-based; so that as enlightenment takes hold, it vibrates or broadcasts out its own frequency, which others so able can receive—so that when one takes hold of enlightenment, they indirectly help others to do the same as well. This is what we call the indirect transference of enlightenment. All Contactees serve this purpose in some form or another. That is one of many facets of what Contactees are all about.

Contactees serve to hold or broadcast the various frequencies, which are being utilized to enlighten modern man, *en masse*. They, the Contactees, may also be thought of as pillars or posts holding up the foundation of this new frequency. They directly act to ground this new frequency as it is being established upon the Earth.

And therein is one of the core reasons, of many, that large numbers of Contactees are genetically altered and programmed psychologically, so as to both hold and maintain this new frequency, acting as anchors or pillars, if you will, so that all of mankind may more readily absorb and maintain this new frequency—that is, the frequency of enlightenment, which we have said many times before is information which has been acquired, integrated, and utilized, or put into practice or use.

Enlightenment is not some kind of new age philosophy or theoretical doctrine; enlightenment is real, and operates in the physical universe the same as do you.

One prime example of this is that Contactees are taught that the Earth is a living, breathing entity. This may seem obvious to some, but many countless people have yet to make that most basic of connections.

Using the above as an example, countless Contactees are programmed both genetically (to house) and psychologically (to maintain) this information. This information is then acquired, integrated, and utilized (put into use) by Contactees everywhere. As this information, more correctly called enlightenment, gets disseminated, it starts to change the general public's perception of the Earth, and its role within the human biological and metaphysical system.

This is just one example; countless others exist, of course, so that as this so-called information-based enlightenment gets disseminated throughout the general populace, it changes people's perception of their surroundings—or, more correctly, it changes the frequency, or the way in which they vibrate. Once again, all existence is frequency-based.

As the frequency at which people vibrate begins to change, this, in and of itself, allows for further and greater change to take place, so that more and greater change (i.e., change to a greater degree) is possible and indeed desirable from our perspective. One facilitates the other: Change allows for, or makes possible, additional or greater change.

An oversimplified example of this might be thought of in terms of how digging a hole allows one to dig a deeper hole, so on and so forth. Before one can have a deeper hole, one first needs a hole.

Our part in all of this—and there are many countless other participants besides ourselves, including those whose job it is to physically contact the Contactees—is a quite simple one, really: to disseminate this type of information.

You see, we are a part of this grand scheme, and our clan or group of participants is all about changing the frequency of man, heretofore called enlightenment.

We want to change the frequency at which man vibrates.

Lastly, don't depend on the opinion of others as you read this information. See within yourself if this information resonates well, for there again, only you can decide for yourself such matters.

GODS OF CREATION

The gods of creation are returning to the Earth at this time—gods or creatures of a higher order, it is all the same. Call it what you will, the creatures responsible for mankind's creation are returning to redirect human evolution.

Humans evolve, of course, but what is less apparent, less understood, is that humans evolve along set parameters. The path upon which human evolution has taken place is a fixed one. Progress—human progress and evolution—is fixed, rather than being random as some might think. There is nothing whatsoever random about the evolution of man. And the evolution of man is nothing if not predictable.

Predictable? Predictable in what way?

Well, predicable in the sense that a baby evolves into adulthood over time. Seen in this light, one would say that the evolution of a child is fixed and predicable; so, too, the evolution of the human species.

Humans are maturing at a faster pace than ever before. Evolution of the species is accelerating ever faster, to the point at which humans now need a newer operational frequency, or operational system, to handle the advanced information stream which is available to them. It is this stream, which will carry human evolution into a higher plane of development and a higher intellectual level from which they are able to operate.

Evolution is a funny thing—far from being random, it follows a preset, predetermined or predefined course (as does the development of a child into adulthood). This preset course takes a species' development ever further into what we refer to simply as the natural progression of enlightenment. Remember, enlightenment is simply the acquisition, integration, and utilization of information. Information must be acquired, integrated, and, in turn, utilized to bring about enlightenment.

What good is information that does not end up being utilized?

This information stream to which we refer is constantly in motion throughout the universe.

It is indeed a stream of information, which is frequency-based. That is to say, it is a physical signal, which does exist and *is* being transmitted from some point within the universe.

This is also what we refer to as the fabric or matrix which exists throughout the universe, upon which other frequencies are connected, based, secured, and fixed, in order to establish a foundation from which to operate these other frequencies, systems, and so forth.

We have surmised that the center of the universe has, as part of its function, the task of broadcasting the creation frequency. Galaxies then relay this frequency (pick up and strengthen this frequency for rebroadcast). This is a universal function of galaxies.

The creation frequency is the fabric of space (now considered dark energy by some at this point in time). Scientists today are starting to realize that there is something within empty space, as they call it, that exists to keep everything in motion, but as of yet, they can't wrap their minds around it.

The creation frequency *is* the fabric or matrix of space—the cohesive element, if you will—which allows for all of existence. There again, we have surmised this, reasoning it out based on probabilities. Perhaps it is best to think of this base frequency as the canvas upon which one would construct their painting. This is logical and understandable science here—but then, it is more advanced, at least at this point in time, than what most mainstream scientists might imagine.

We say all of this so that one might understand that there is no mysterious, unobtainable force at work here, but science of the kind with which you are familiar.

The same science which exists now existed two hundred years ago, but it was mostly unknown or unimagined at that point in history. Today, the average 8th-grader knows far more science than even the most gifted of scientists some hundred years ago.

Evolution—the evolution of the species, en masse—continues onward. Not all evolution of the various species existing on this planet involves shepherding by creatures of a higher order, but many do. Why is it that some creatures have changed (evolved) little over hundreds of millions of years, and yet others have changed drastically over tens of thousands of years? If all evolution was a natural process, all creatures would evolve along a uniform path, no? Well, that doesn't happen, does it? Creatures evolve based upon input (or the lack thereof) from creatures of a higher order.

Man's evolutionary path has been a very convoluted one, manipulated by many creatures, many *types* of creatures of a higher order. To wit, we would like to point to one seemingly insignificant aspect of man's presence on this planet in order to shed light on his having been shepherded throughout his evolution.

Why is it that humans continually seek a god, or gods?

The answer is that genetically, humans are predisposed to seeking out a god or gods. This is a specific genetic program, programmed into humans for a specific purpose.

Let's think about this for a moment – humans seek out a god, or gods, not randomly, but because they are programmed to exhibit this behavior. Humans are predisposed to exhibit this behavior—*genetically* predisposed to exhibit this behavior.

Yes, indeed: this is a specific behavior pattern that exists in humans because (and *only* because) it was specifically designed into humans via genetic programing.

You see, if it weren't for this genetically- based behavior pattern, humans would simply go about doing what they do, and that would be that. So first you have the genetic predisposition for a specific behavior pattern (e.g., seeking a god or god's figurehead), and then you have the means (religion in *all* of its various iterations), which literally plugs into that genetic trait.

So, what we are saying here is that creatures of a higher order (your gods, if you wish) genetically programmed you for the specific behavior pattern of seeking out a god or gods, then provided the various religions which you are able to fulfill or plug into based upon that specific genetic programming.

This all just didn't come about by accident.

Long ago you were programmed—genetically programmed—to exhibit this behavior, and you do; and in turn, you now see your life, your world, the universe, all based upon this behavior.

THE BIGGEST CRIME
AGAINST MANKIND

From our perspective, the biggest crime against mankind has been relegating the human thought process to what we would call dualistic thinking.

<u>Dualistic Thinking</u>

Dualistic thinking puts everything encountered into an either-or, right-or-wrong scenario, so that you are left with only two choices—either something is right or it's wrong; either it's good or it's bad; either it makes sense or it doesn't. There's no middle ground to be found. What that does is eliminate all thought processes that would shade or color issues and the information being processed by the mind into the various categories which actually exist. By eliminating that capability within mankind, what they've done is relegate man to a narrow band of perception.

And this is insidious. Imagine that you could only see two colors, pure black and pure white. All the other colors of the rainbow are not available to you, because you were genetically programmed—set up, created to function—only seeing things in pure black, or pure white; no shades of gray, no colors or their various hues. How would that affect your perception of the world around you? Either something was black, pure black, or white, pure white. How would you see the world around you, the universe, everything that existed within your realm of perception?

How would you see that?

Once you see this in that connotation, you can understand that it's quite limiting overall.

And even as you read this now, perhaps you're thinking "This is right" or "This is wrong". So, the question then is, how do you get out of this dualistic thought process—that good-or-bad, right-or-wrong, yes-or-no, thought process?

This, more than anything, is what has limited man's intellect throughout the ages: this dualistic thought process that you'll find in a lot of religious doctrines and religious texts. You'll find that good/bad, God/Satan mentality, which gets transferred to everything within the human experience. This, more than anything else, is what has limited human intellect. It's not the human brain; the human brain has a capacity far greater than what is being utilized. And even scientists, your scientists today, realize that the brain exists in such a way that it's really underutilized.

This one aspect of your thought process—dualistic thinking, good or bad, right or wrong, yes or no—has hindered you, has kept human progress at pretty much a crawl.

So how do you go on from here? Where do you go from here? How do you change any aspect of this?

You can't. All you can do is recognize it—that is to say, recognize that you are programmed. You are genetically predisposed to thinking in terms of right or wrong, pure black and pure white—no in-between whatsoever. So, once you see that, you can say, "Okay, I am predisposed to having this happen. I am predisposed to thinking this way. I am predisposed to living this way." Once you recognize it—that aspect of that understanding—you are freed from that. That's not to say that you won't think in those terms, or that you're more likely to think in those terms than not. What it means is that you'll see it; you'll understand it for what it is, and you'll understand why you were genetically programmed this way: to limit your understanding, to limit your evolutionary progress, your evolution as a creature of the universe. And with that understanding, you can proceed on.

It really depends on you being reprogrammed genetically, more than even seeing it—and ultimately, that's what we are here to do, is to reprogram the human species genetically so as to see in all of the colors, shades, and hues of the rainbow.

THE SUBMISSIVE DOCTRINE

Mankind, as part of its programming, has been taught to be submissive to its gods. Integrated and hidden throughout all of the various doctrines and religious texts spread throughout the world is what we call the Submissive Doctrine, whereby all of mankind is encouraged to be submissive with regard to their gods or creatures designated as beings of a higher power.

They, for the most part, all teach that you are worthless sinners (and going so far to say that you were born into sin), or all destined for a life of pain, and all unworthy for anything but the trash heap.

Why is that?

You are splendid, beautiful creatures of the universe, not trash. This was done on purpose, or with a particular purpose in mind, and that purpose was to keep mankind submissive, both conceptually and within its thought processes, with regard to those creatures it considers to be its gods—whatever their names.

Logically, why would any creature of a higher order want you submissive to it? Creatures of a higher order are naturally beyond that petty concept.

Logically, wouldn't it rather have you enlightened and on the fast track of evolution based on information, so as to help and care for your own species—in effect, self-supporting?

Information breeds enlightenment; enlightenment breeds evolution of the species, which then provides the means for the species to better serve itself.

Put in the context of children, why on Earth would you as a father or mother want your child held back from its evolution (and learning process) into adulthood? The answer is you wouldn't...period!

All creatures throughout the universe are rooting for you to evolve to a higher order.

You see, there is nothing good about this Submissive Doctrine as implemented; it is insidious at its core and has kept mankind under thumb and ignorant to a large extent.

Under the guise of a paternal father figure, brother, or maternal mother figure, it purports to show mankind 'The Way', when in reality, it keeps mankind submissive to the very doctrines which trumpet themselves as helping mankind. This is what we call a closed loop, in that it both feeds on and supports itself.

Once again, this is insidious and destructive to the well-being of man. It is only designed for the benefit of those that would profit from man in no small way. And it was designed for ease of implementation from generation to generations, i.e., passed down from generation to generation through family units via all of the various major religious doctrines throughout the world.

To wit: To even suggest that this is the case is to be considered heresy—blasphemy against God, capital G.

It's brilliant in its execution, no doubt, but detrimental to mankind, of course. And it impedes mankind's evolution into the frequency of information or enlightenment, as we prefer to call it. Remember, this is all about keeping information from mankind, in effect saying, "You don't need information; focus on these religious doctrines instead." This is especially noticeable in the Middle East, and even more so in other, less evolved areas of the world.

Ask yourself: Why is it that these religious doctrines disempowered man?

The universe, after all, is all about empowerment through information.

RELIGION VS. THE UNIVERSE

With regard to mankind, it has always been about religion and the various religious doctrines spread throughout the world versus the universe—or information, which the universe is. One could also make the argument that it has always been about religion versus science, for science at its most basic is all about understanding the universe and how things function within the universe.

Looking throughout mankind's recorded history, it's easy to see that religion has always impeded science. At every step of the way, religion has continually been challenging science, forcing it to integrate into its worldview—always holding science at bay every step of the way until the evidence from science (evidence slow in coming), was so overwhelming, so overwhelmingly profound, as to make its way into the religiously-based worldview mandatory. Then, and only then, does religion give way, finding some obscure text or passage that is often changed to fit the way science says it is—in effect saying, "Wait, this is what the texts have said all along, and see, they really do fit", but always after the fact, it seems.

There again, looking over the last several thousand years of man's history, it's obvious that over and over again, religion has impeded science (which is basically information about the universe and how it operates) so as to slow mankind's progression into the knowledge of science—and so, too, the universe, which once again, is all about information, or as we prefer to call it, enlightenment.

Why is that?

Think about this for a moment: Perhaps there are some that have wanted you this way—ignorant, for the most part. But the universe, and all of the information therein, was designed for the benefit of all creatures. How then can any creatures, whether beings of a higher order or not, hold back the information, which is the universe?

Who can hold back the universe?

Well, *they* can—and did, in your case—but not for long, as it turns out. Humans are becoming enlightened—enlightened creatures coming into the fold, as it were, of the information, which is the universe.

Made in the USA
Middletown, DE
13 June 2023

32542229R00031